CAPTAIN ECO
AND THE FATE OF THE
EARTH

Written by
Jonathon Porritt

Illustrated by
Ellis Nadler

DORLING KINDERSLEY, INC.

NEW YORK

*For Eleanor,
and Fred Bush*

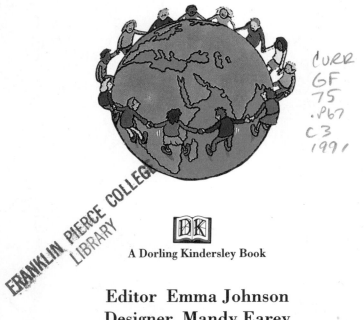

A Dorling Kindersley Book

Editor Emma Johnson
Designer Mandy Earey
Production Marguerite Fenn
Art Director Roger Priddy

Type by Jack Potter
and Terry Christien
Research by Stephen Webster

First American Edition, 1991
10 9 8 7 6 5 4 3 2 1

Dorling Kindersley, Inc., 232 Madison Avenue
New York, New York 10016

ISBN 1-879431-12-2
ISBN 1-879431-27-0 (lib. bdg.)

Library of Congress Catalog Card Number 91-060142

Color reproduction by Dot Gradations, Essex
Printed and bound in Britain on Sylvan Coat recycled paper by
BPCC Hazell Books, Bristol

CONTENTS

IMAGINE A HISTORY BOOK WRITTEN IN THE YEAR 2040...

THE MODERN AGE
(1995 TO THE PRESENT DAY)

AFTER MORE THAN 200 YEARS OF "INDUSTRIAL PROGRESS," IT DAWNED ON PEOPLE THAT THEY HAD STOPPED PROGRESSING ALTOGETHER, SIMPLY BECAUSE THEY HAD MADE SUCH A MESS OF THE EARTH. OTHER PEOPLE STILL REFUSED TO SEE THE PROBLEMS OR CHANGE THEIR WAYS. THE EARTH JUST COULDN'T COPE. ITS NATURAL RESOURCES WERE BEING DEPLETED QUICKLY.

BUT, TOWARDS THE END OF THE 1990s, THINGS BEGAN TO CHANGE. THE YOUNGER GENERATION LOOKED AT THE WORLD THEY WERE ABOUT TO INHERIT AND DIDN'T LIKE IT ONE BIT. THEY BEGAN TO WORK TOGETHER, AND TO TALK ABOUT SOLUTIONS TO MANY DIFFERENT ENVIRONMENTAL PROBLEMS. THEY WERE DETERMINED TO LIVE DIFFERENTLY THAN THEIR PARENTS, TO PROTECT THE EARTH AND ALL THAT LIVED HERE.

POLITICIANS HAD NO CHOICE BUT TO SUPPORT THE "GREEN" MOVEMENT OR STEP ASIDE. SCIENTISTS WORKED TOGETHER TO FIND WAYS OF MEETING PEOPLE'S NEEDS WITHOUT DAMAGING THE EARTH. RELIGIOUS HATRED AND POLITICAL DIFFERENCES WERE SET ASIDE TO MEET THIS ENORMOUS CHALLENGE— THE MOST IMPORTANT TASK THE HUMAN RACE HAD EVER FACED.

IT WASN'T EASY, BUT BIT BY BIT THE YOUNGER GENERATION ADOPTED ANOTHER PURPOSE FOR THE HUMAN SPECIES: TO ACT AS GUARDIANS AND CARETAKERS OF ALL LIFE ON EARTH,

AND HERE'S HOW IT ALL BEGAN...

6

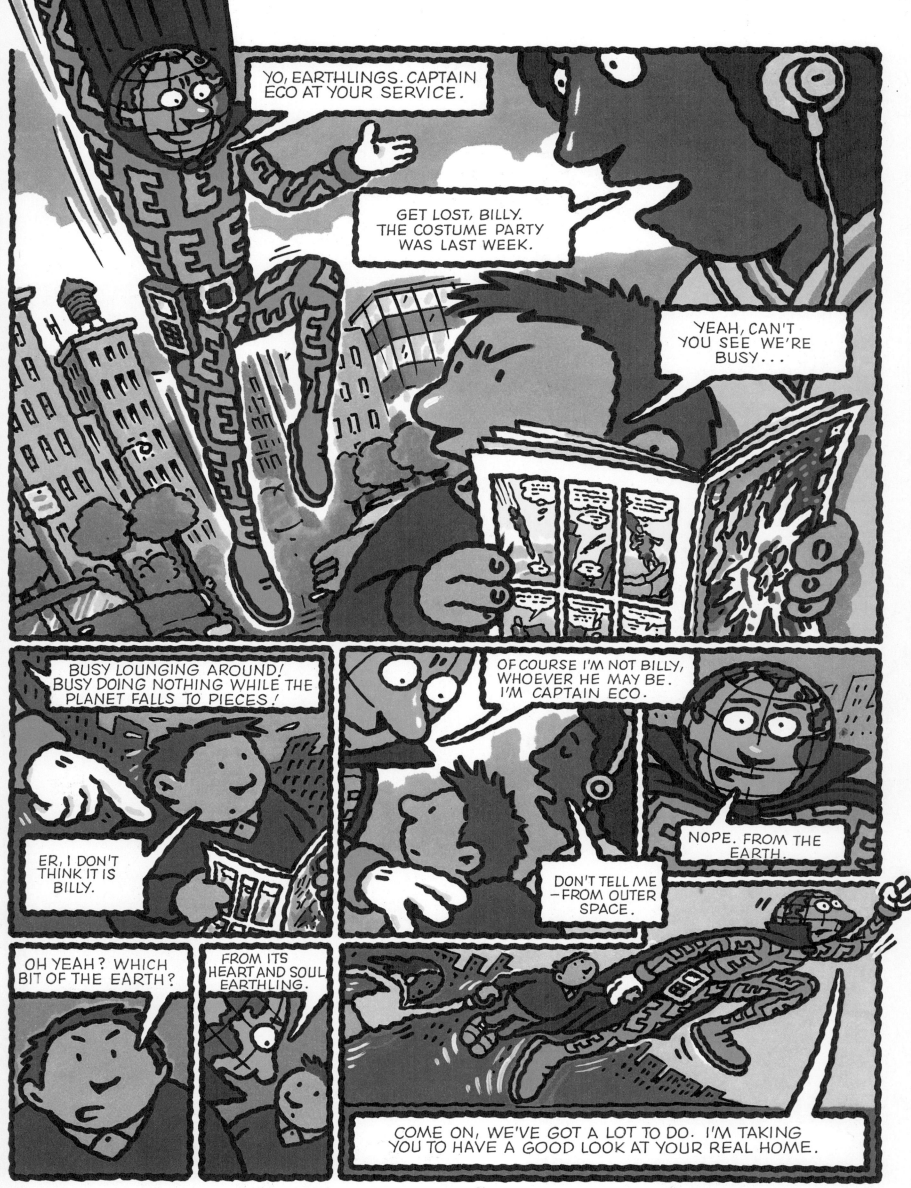

A HISTORY OF THE EARTH

IN TWO PAGES

OH YES, MILLIONS OF YOU ARE BETTER OFF. BUT WHAT'S THE POINT OF GETTING RICHER IF YOU'RE KILLING THE PLANET?

IT CAN'T LAST. FOR ALL YOUR COMPUTERS AND ZAPPY GADGETS, AND YOUR BRILLIANT SCIENTISTS AND WHIZ KIDS, YOU'D BE NOWHERE WITHOUT THE EARTH'S NATURAL RESOURCES—ITS ENERGY, MINERALS, TREES, RIVERS, THE SOIL ITSELF.

IF YOU DESTROY THESE THINGS, YOU DESTROY YOURSELVES!

SINCE 1850 THE WORLD POPULATION HAS GROWN FROM 1 BILLION TO 5 BILLION. THAT'S OVER 170,000 PER YEAR.

ONE SPECIES OF ANIMAL DISAPPEARS EVERY HALF HOUR.

YOU'VE USED AS MUCH COAL IN THE LAST 50 YEARS AS IN THE WHOLE OF HISTORY TO DATE.

IN THE LAST 150 YEARS, 70,000 NEW CHEMICALS HAVE BEEN RELEASED INTO THE ENVIRONMENT.

EVERY DAY 40,000 CHILDREN DIE OF DISEASES THAT COULD EASILY BE PREVENTED.

BUT WE'VE GOT TO GET RICHER IF WE'RE GOING TO BE ABLE TO SORT THINGS OUT.

YOU'RE JUST TRYING TO SCARE US, LIKE GREENPEACE...

THAT'S WHAT YOU EARTHLINGS HAVE ALWAYS SAID. BUT FOR EVERY PROBLEM SOLVED ANOTHER ONE POPS UP.

..OR THOSE FIENDS OF THE EARTH I'VE SEEN ON T.V.

FRIENDS OF THE EARTH, I THINK YOU'LL FIND.

SAME DIFFERENCE. ANYWAY, WHAT'S IT GOT TO DO WITH US?

IT'S YOUR FUTURE WE'RE TALKING ABOUT.

YES THERE IS! EVEN YOU CAN DO SOMETHING, CHRIS.

BUT THERE'S NOTHING WE CAN DO ABOUT IT, IS THERE?

WATCH IT!

BUT FIRST YOU'VE GOT TO UNDERSTAND WHERE THE EARTH'S ENERGY COMES FROM.

BURN, BURN, BURN

YOU NEED ENERGY TO LIVE. THE BUSIER YOU ARE THE MORE ENERGY YOU USE. YOU EARTHLINGS GOT WHERE YOU ARE TODAY BY BURNING THINGS. FIRST IT WAS FIREWOOD.

THAT WAS THE ONLY SOURCE OF ENERGY FOR MOST OF THE 100,000 YEARS YOU'VE BEEN AROUND. THEN IT WAS COAL.

THEN OIL AND NATURAL GAS.

ALL OF THESE FORMS OF ENERGY — WOOD, COAL, OIL AND GAS — ARE GIVEN TO US BY THE SUN. AS TREES GROW, THEY STORE UP ENERGY; WHEN THEY'RE BURNED, THE ENERGY IS RELEASED.

BORING! WE DID THIS AT SCHOOL TOO. "COAL, OIL AND GAS ARE KNOWN AS 'FOSSIL FUELS', BECAUSE THEY'RE MADE UP OF FOSSILIZED PLANTS AND ANIMALS THAT DECOMPOSED MILLIONS OF YEARS AGO".

EXACTLY! BUT YOU EARTHLINGS ARE NOW TOTALLY DEPENDENT ON FOSSIL FUELS. INDUSTRY, TRANSPORTATION, AGRICULTURE: THE WHEELS GO AROUND SIMPLY BECAUSE YOU'VE LEARNED HOW TO DIG UP THIS STORE OF ENERGY AND BURN IT. BUT YOU'RE HOOKED. YOU'VE BECOME OIL JUNKIES.

BUT THERE'S LOADS OF OIL LEFT. IT'S NOT GOING TO RUN OUT FOR A LONG TIME IS IT?

IT DEPENDS HOW CAREFULLY YOU USE WHAT'S LEFT. AND WHAT ABOUT YOUR CHILDREN AND GRANDCHILDREN?

BUT WHAT'S THE PROBLEM, IF WE'RE CAREFUL?

ECO FACTS

IN JUST ONE YEAR, EARTHLINGS BURN UP COAL, OIL AND GAS THAT TOOK A MILLION YEARS TO FORM.

10

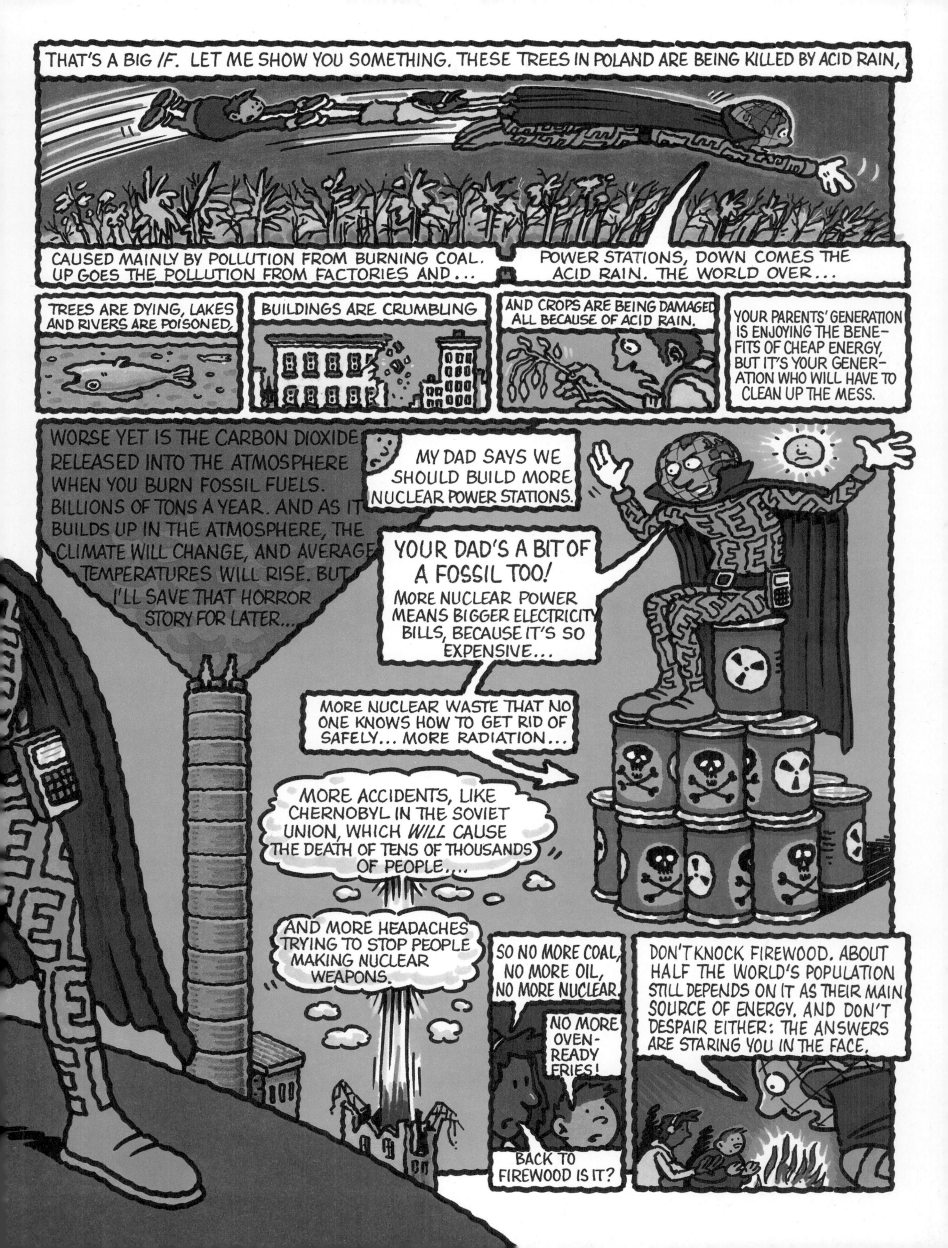

ENERGY FOR EVER AND EVER

...WELL, ALMOST

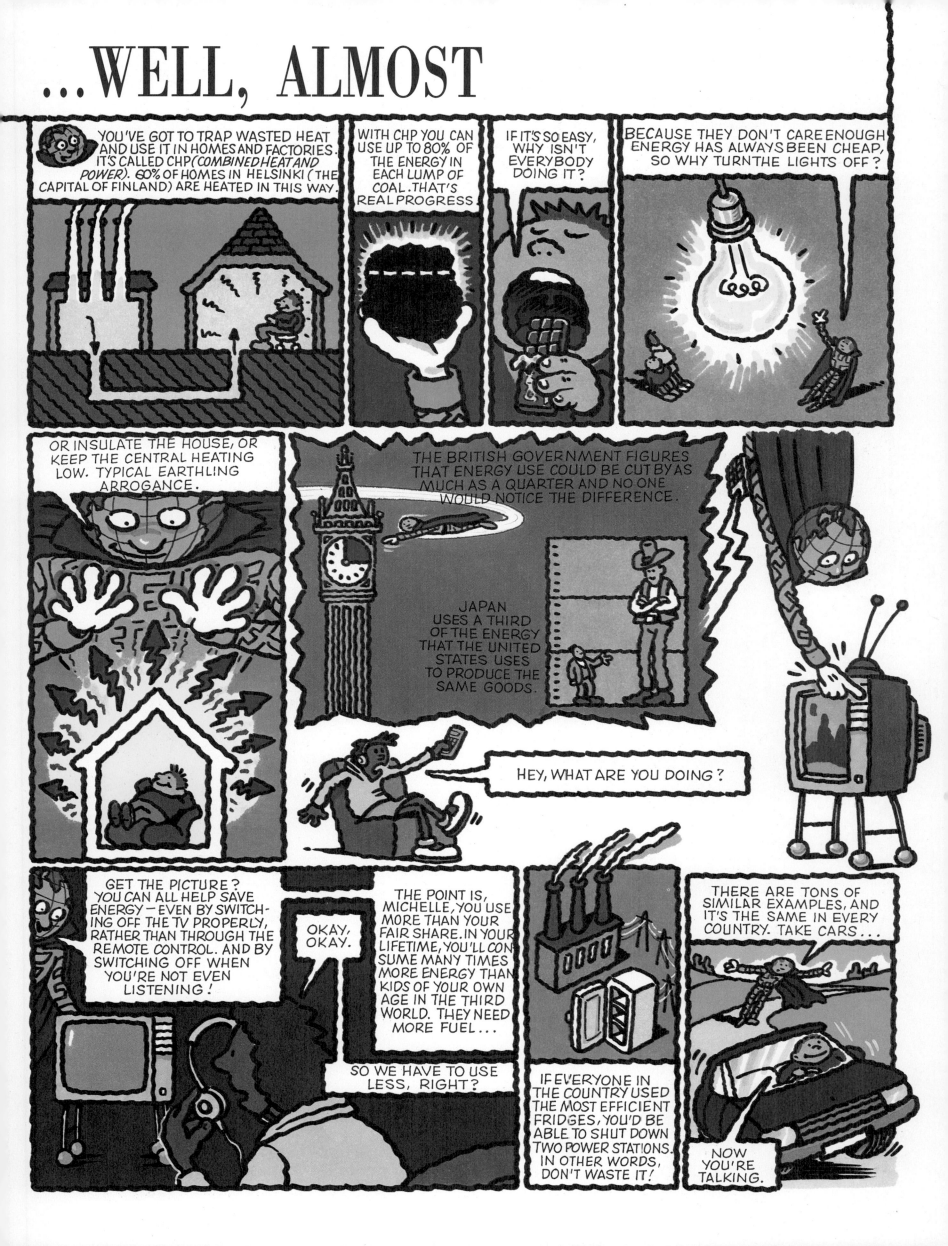

CARS, CARS, CARS

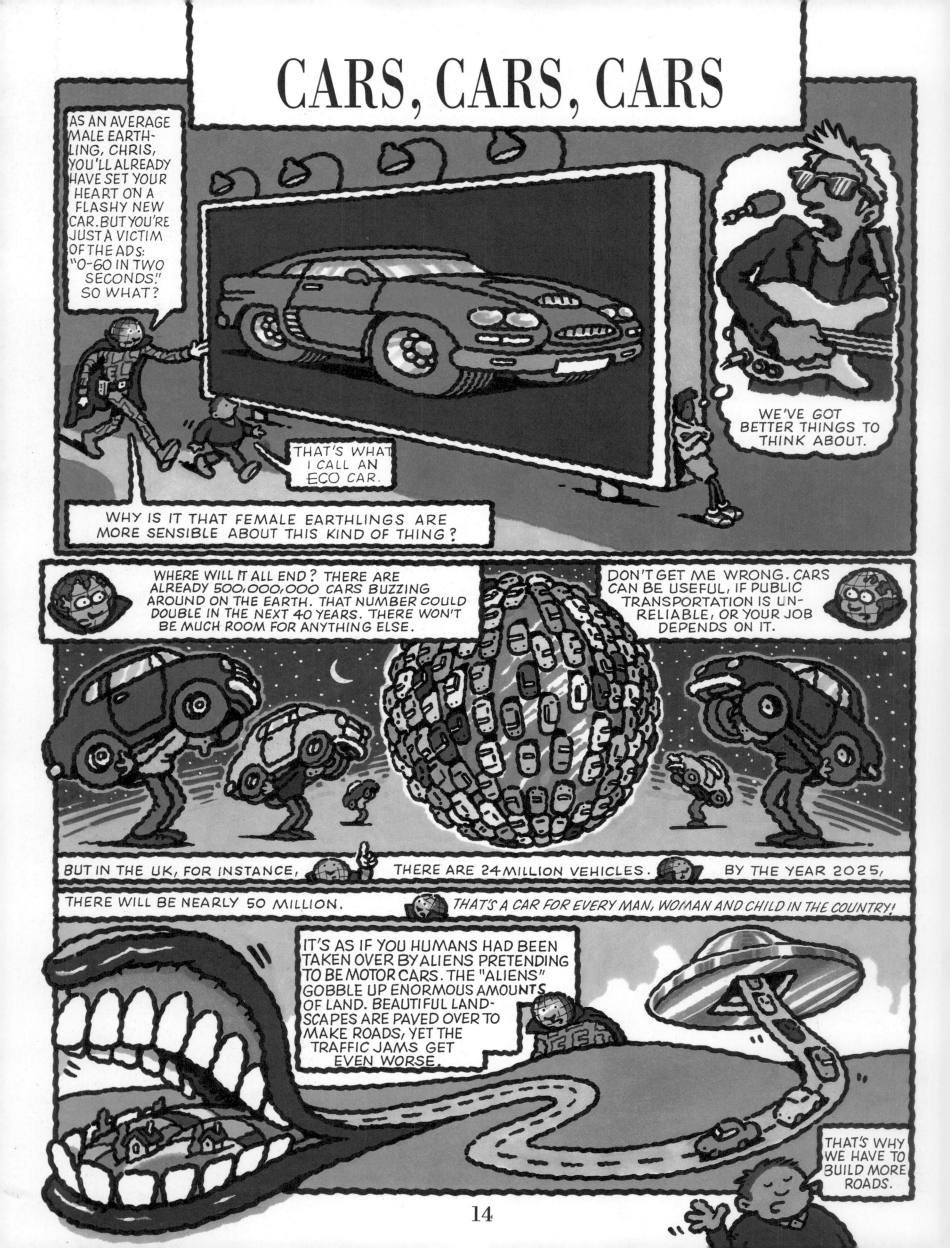

AS AN AVERAGE MALE EARTH-LING, CHRIS, YOU'LL ALREADY HAVE SET YOUR HEART ON A FLASHY NEW CAR. BUT YOU'RE JUST A VICTIM OF THE ADS: "0-60 IN TWO SECONDS!" SO WHAT?

WE'VE GOT BETTER THINGS TO THINK ABOUT.

THAT'S WHAT I CALL AN ECO CAR.

WHY IS IT THAT FEMALE EARTHLINGS ARE MORE SENSIBLE ABOUT THIS KIND OF THING?

WHERE WILL IT ALL END? THERE ARE ALREADY 500,000,000 CARS BUZZING AROUND ON THE EARTH. THAT NUMBER COULD DOUBLE IN THE NEXT 40 YEARS. THERE WON'T BE MUCH ROOM FOR ANYTHING ELSE.

DON'T GET ME WRONG. CARS CAN BE USEFUL, IF PUBLIC TRANSPORTATION IS UN-RELIABLE, OR YOUR JOB DEPENDS ON IT.

BUT IN THE UK, FOR INSTANCE, THERE ARE 24 MILLION VEHICLES. BY THE YEAR 2025, THERE WILL BE NEARLY 50 MILLION. THAT'S A CAR FOR EVERY MAN, WOMAN AND CHILD IN THE COUNTRY!

IT'S AS IF YOU HUMANS HAD BEEN TAKEN OVER BY ALIENS PRETENDING TO BE MOTOR CARS. THE "ALIENS" GOBBLE UP ENORMOUS AMOUNTS OF LAND. BEAUTIFUL LAND-SCAPES ARE PAVED OVER TO MAKE ROADS, YET THE TRAFFIC JAMS GET EVEN WORSE.

THAT'S WHY WE HAVE TO BUILD MORE ROADS.

14

TRAVELING GREEN

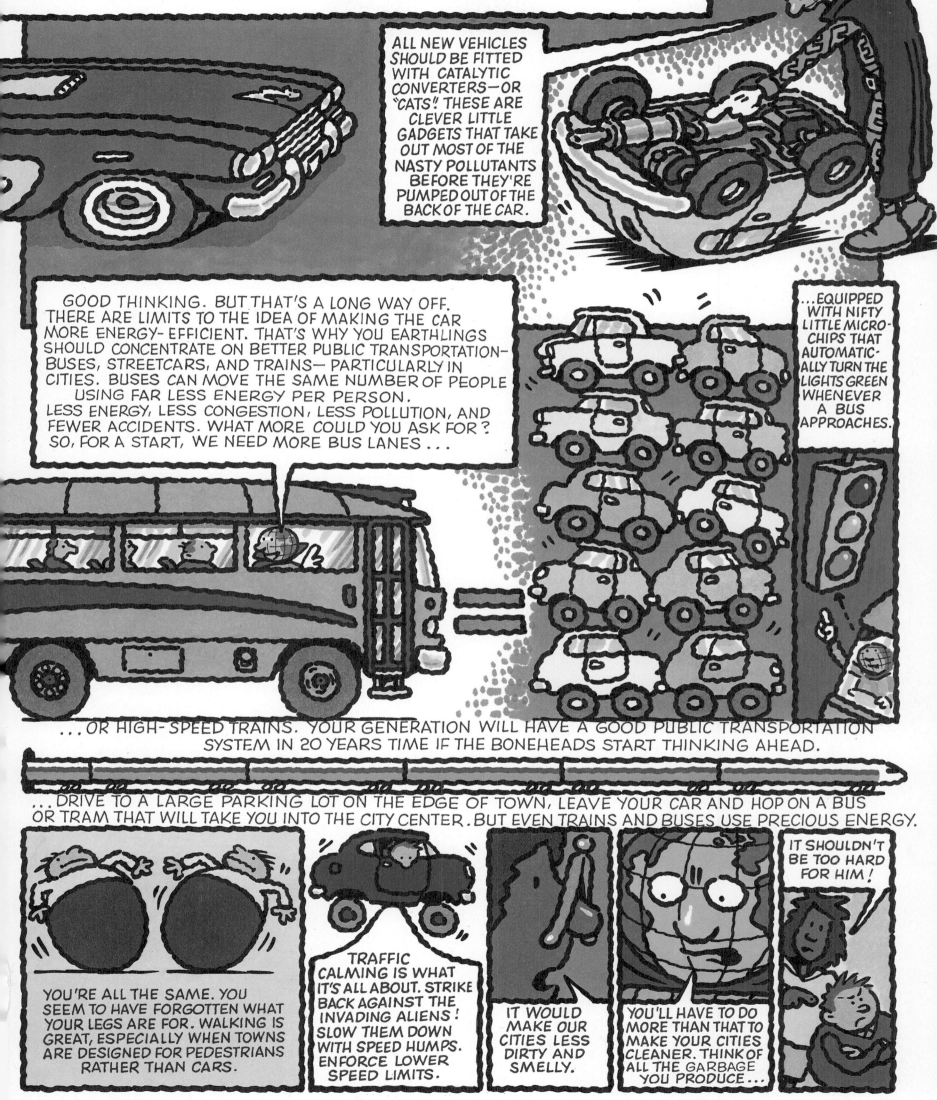

TALKING GARBAGE

HOW MUCH DO YOU WEIGH, CHRIS?

77 POUNDS, I THINK.

ON A GOOD DAY.

IN ONE YEAR, AN AVERAGE PERSON IN THE USA OR EUROPE PRODUCES AS MUCH GARBAGE AS 300 CHRISES. SOME OF IT IS THE STUFF YOU THROW AWAY AT HOME, BUT IT'S ALSO THE WASTE CREATED BY SHOPS, FACTORIES RESTAURANTS, OFFICES, AND OTHER BUSINESSES.

300 CHRISES WORTH OF GAR-BAGE MAKES YOU THINK.

AND MOST OF IT GOES INTO *HUGE HOLES* IN THE GROUND CALLED "LANDFILLS."

SOME AMERICAN CITIES HAVE ALREADY RUN OUT OF HOLES, SO THEY HAVE TO TRANSPORT THEIR GARBAGE THOUSANDS OF MILES TO PLACES WHERE THERE ARE STILL SOME HOLES LEFT.

WHAT HAPPENS WHEN THEY'RE FULL UP?

NO ONE'S THOUGHT OF THAT. IN THE MEANTIME, THESE DUMPS CAN BE DANGEROUS, BECAUSE THEY TEND TO LEAK. THE POLITICIANS JUST DON'T WANT TO KNOW ABOUT IT. OUT OF SIGHT, OUT OF MIND—OR SO THEY THINK.

BUT LIKE THE MONSTER FROM THE SWAMP, THE GARBAGE KEEPS COMING BACK TO HAUNT THEM, *AND* IT'S THREATENING TO POISON YOUR WATER

VOTE FOR MR CLEAN

YOU'VE ALWAYS BEEN A DIRTY BUNCH, BUT IT'S GETTING WORSE!

WASTE NOT, WANT NOT

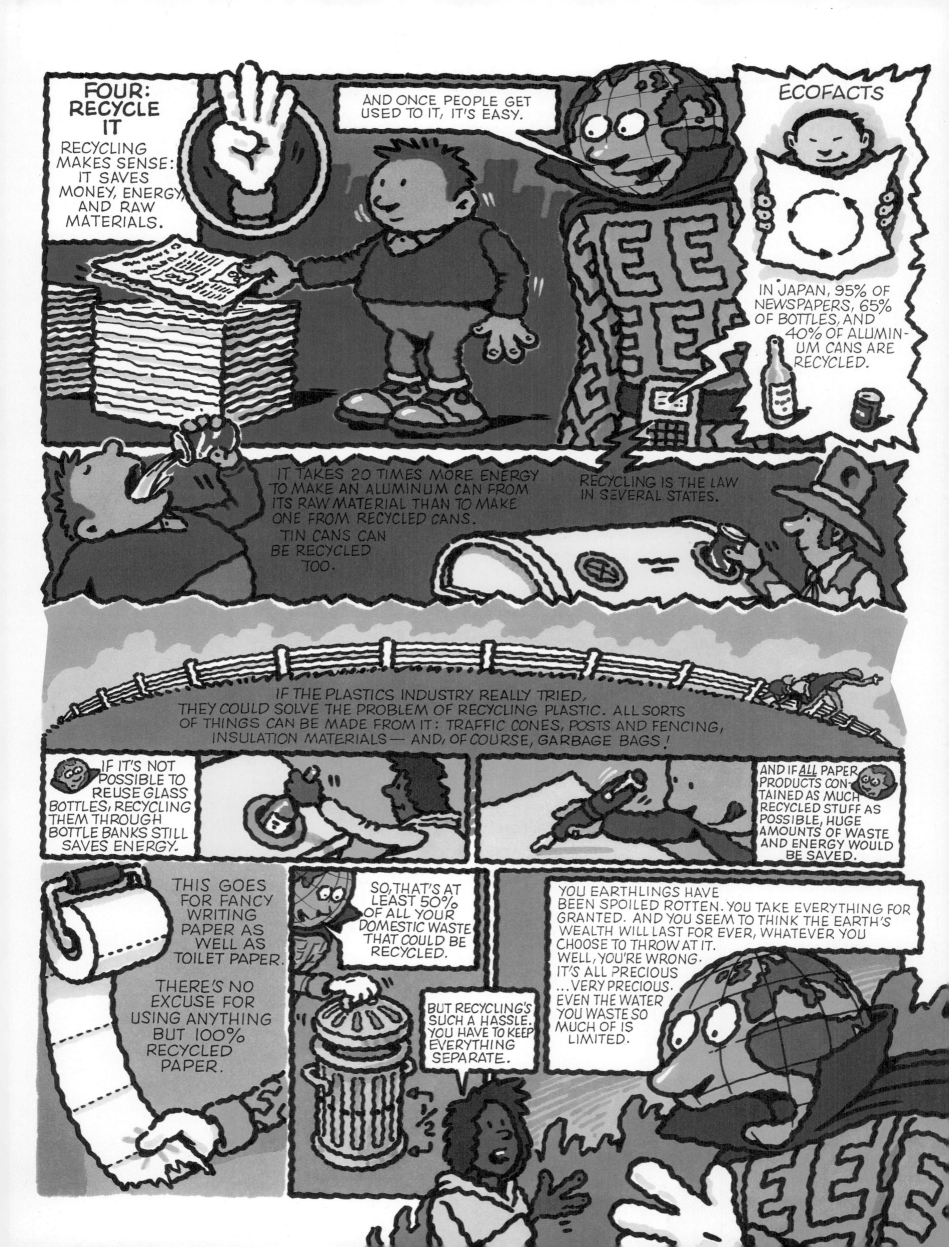

TROUBLED WATERS

ECOFACTS:

THE AVERAGE FAMILY OF FOUR USES ABOUT 900 GALLONS OF WATER EVERY WEEK. AT 3 GALLONS A FLUSH, FLUSHING THE TOILET ACCOUNTS FOR AT LEAST 264 GALLONS!

IT TAKES 100,000 GALLONS TO PRODUCE A CAR.

AND 1,000 GALLONS TO PRODUCE JUST 1 POUND OF BEEF.

HUGE QUANTITIES OF WATER ARE WASTED, WITH NO THOUGHT FOR THE FUTURE. IN PARTS OF THE USA AND EUROPE, CLEAN FRESH WATER IS ALREADY RUNNING OUT. THEN WHERE WILL YOU ALL BE?

WATER IS SUCH PRECIOUS STUFF. YOU NOT ONLY WASTE IT, YOU POLLUTE IT AND POISON IT TOO. INDUSTRY HAS BEEN KILLING RIVERS FOR HUNDREDS OF YEARS. TAKE THE RHINE— ONE OF THE DIRTIEST RIVERS IN EUROPE. BY THE TIME IT REACHES ROTTERDAM IN HOLLAND, IT CONTAINS OVER 50,000 CHEMICALS. AS A RIVER, IT'S JUST ABOUT DEAD.

AND IT'S THE SAME SAD STORY WITH YOUR BEACHES. SOME ARE NOW SO POLLUTED WITH SEWAGE AND OTHER MUCK THAT PEOPLE HAVE TO BE WARNED OFF SWIMMING.

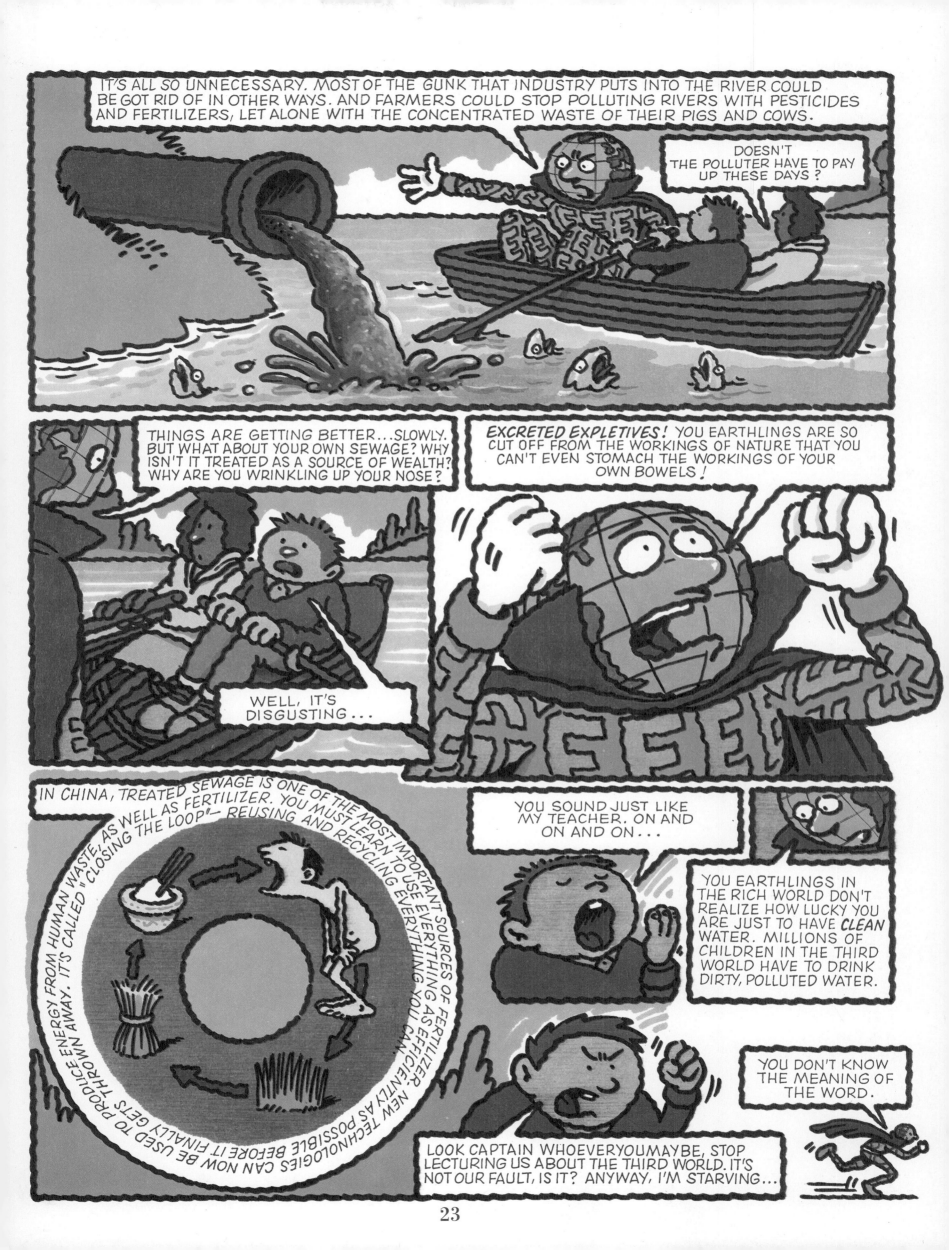

YOU ARE WHAT YOU EAT

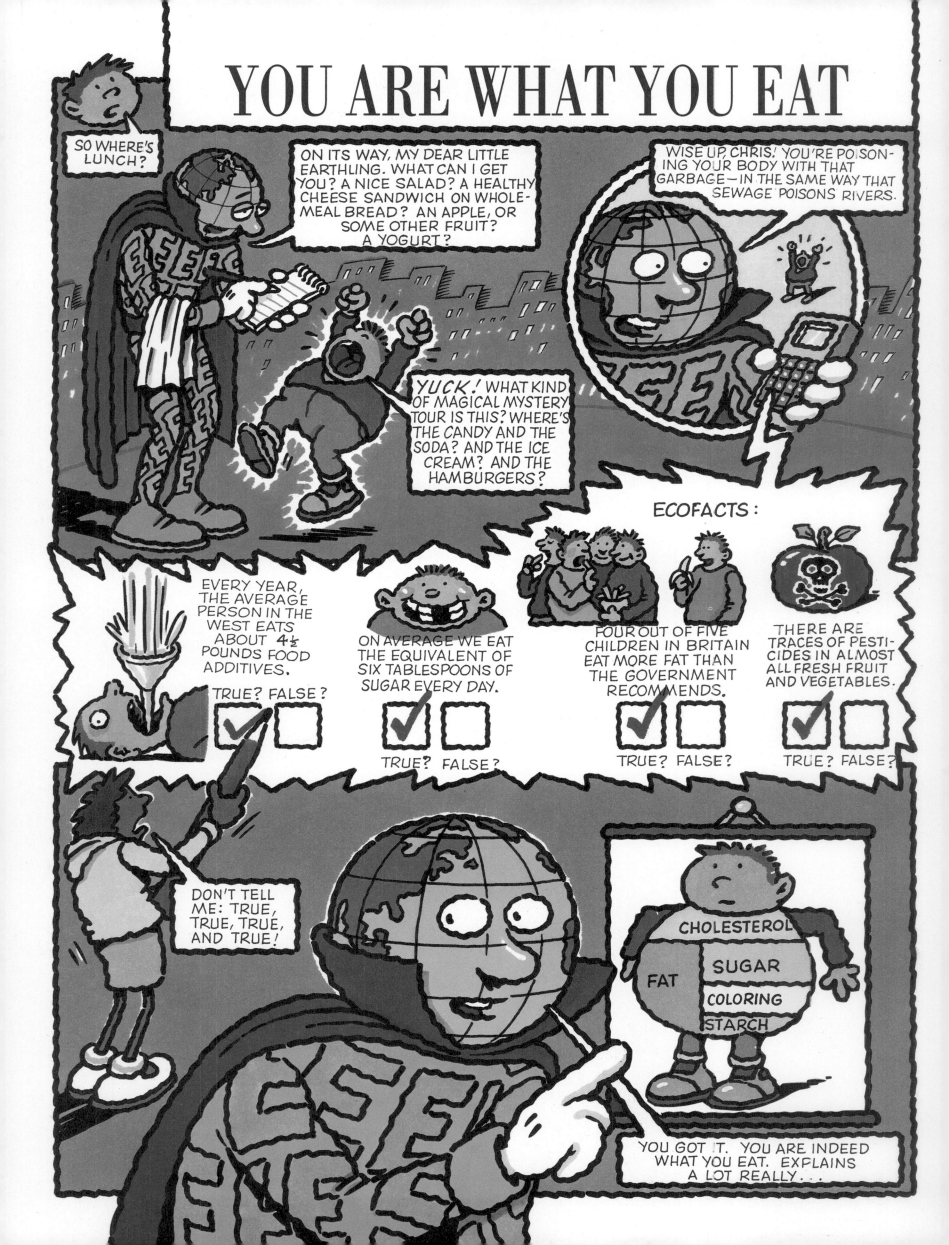

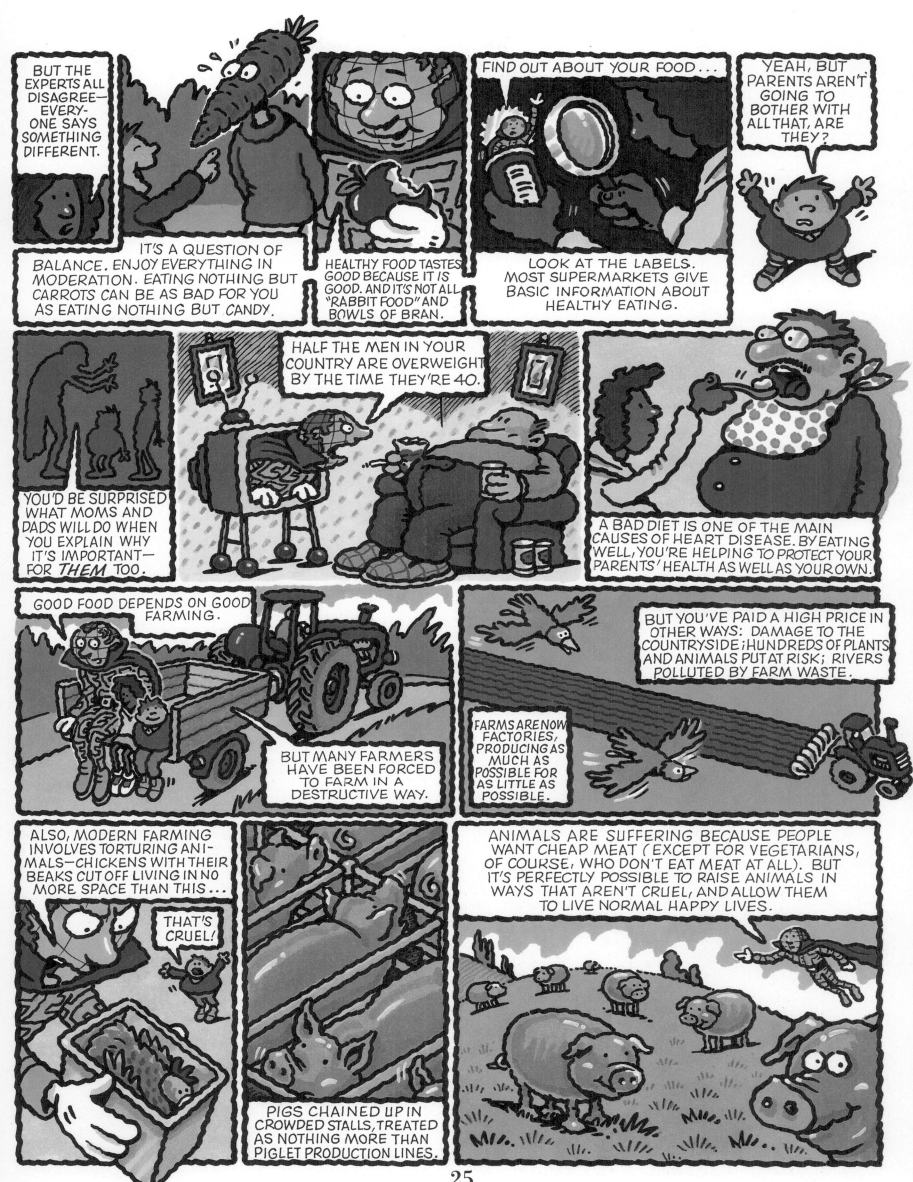

BUT THE EXPERTS ALL DISAGREE—EVERYONE SAYS SOMETHING DIFFERENT.

IT'S A QUESTION OF BALANCE. ENJOY EVERYTHING IN MODERATION. EATING NOTHING BUT CARROTS CAN BE AS BAD FOR YOU AS EATING NOTHING BUT CANDY.

HEALTHY FOOD TASTES GOOD BECAUSE IT IS GOOD. AND IT'S NOT ALL "RABBIT FOOD" AND BOWLS OF BRAN.

FIND OUT ABOUT YOUR FOOD...

LOOK AT THE LABELS. MOST SUPERMARKETS GIVE BASIC INFORMATION ABOUT HEALTHY EATING.

YEAH, BUT PARENTS AREN'T GOING TO BOTHER WITH ALL THAT, ARE THEY?

YOU'D BE SURPRISED WHAT MOMS AND DADS WILL DO WHEN YOU EXPLAIN WHY IT'S IMPORTANT— FOR THEM TOO.

HALF THE MEN IN YOUR COUNTRY ARE OVERWEIGHT BY THE TIME THEY'RE 40.

A BAD DIET IS ONE OF THE MAIN CAUSES OF HEART DISEASE. BY EATING WELL, YOU'RE HELPING TO PROTECT YOUR PARENTS' HEALTH AS WELL AS YOUR OWN.

GOOD FOOD DEPENDS ON GOOD FARMING.

BUT MANY FARMERS HAVE BEEN FORCED TO FARM IN A DESTRUCTIVE WAY.

BUT YOU'VE PAID A HIGH PRICE IN OTHER WAYS: DAMAGE TO THE COUNTRYSIDE; HUNDREDS OF PLANTS AND ANIMALS PUT AT RISK; RIVERS POLLUTED BY FARM WASTE.

FARMS ARE NOW FACTORIES, PRODUCING AS MUCH AS POSSIBLE FOR AS LITTLE AS POSSIBLE.

ALSO, MODERN FARMING INVOLVES TORTURING ANIMALS—CHICKENS WITH THEIR BEAKS CUT OFF LIVING IN NO MORE SPACE THAN THIS...

THAT'S CRUEL!

PIGS CHAINED UP IN CROWDED STALLS, TREATED AS NOTHING MORE THAN PIGLET PRODUCTION LINES.

ANIMALS ARE SUFFERING BECAUSE PEOPLE WANT CHEAP MEAT (EXCEPT FOR VEGETARIANS, OF COURSE, WHO DON'T EAT MEAT AT ALL). BUT IT'S PERFECTLY POSSIBLE TO RAISE ANIMALS IN WAYS THAT AREN'T CRUEL, AND ALLOW THEM TO LIVE NORMAL HAPPY LIVES.

26

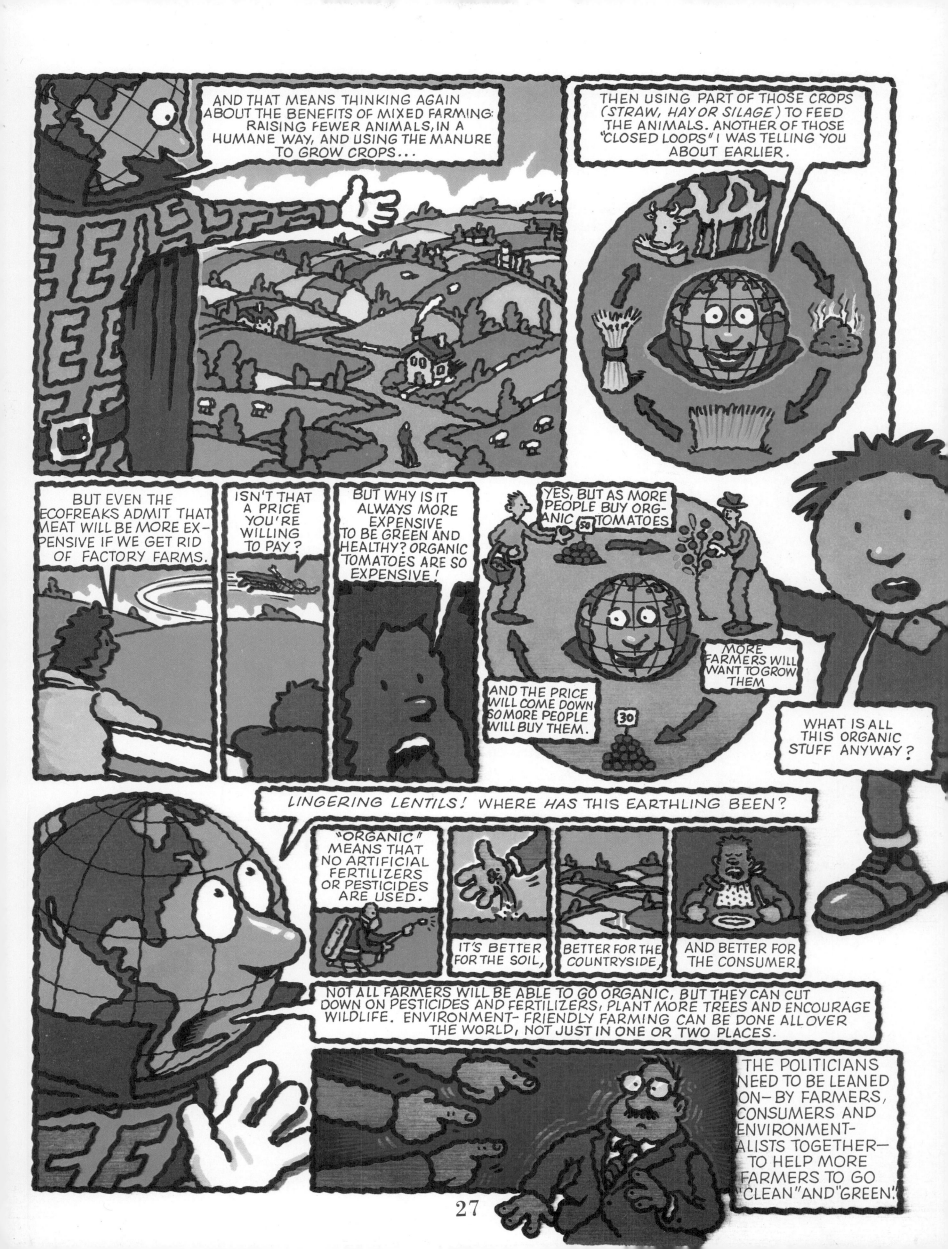

ANIMAL RIGHTS, ANIMAL WRONGS

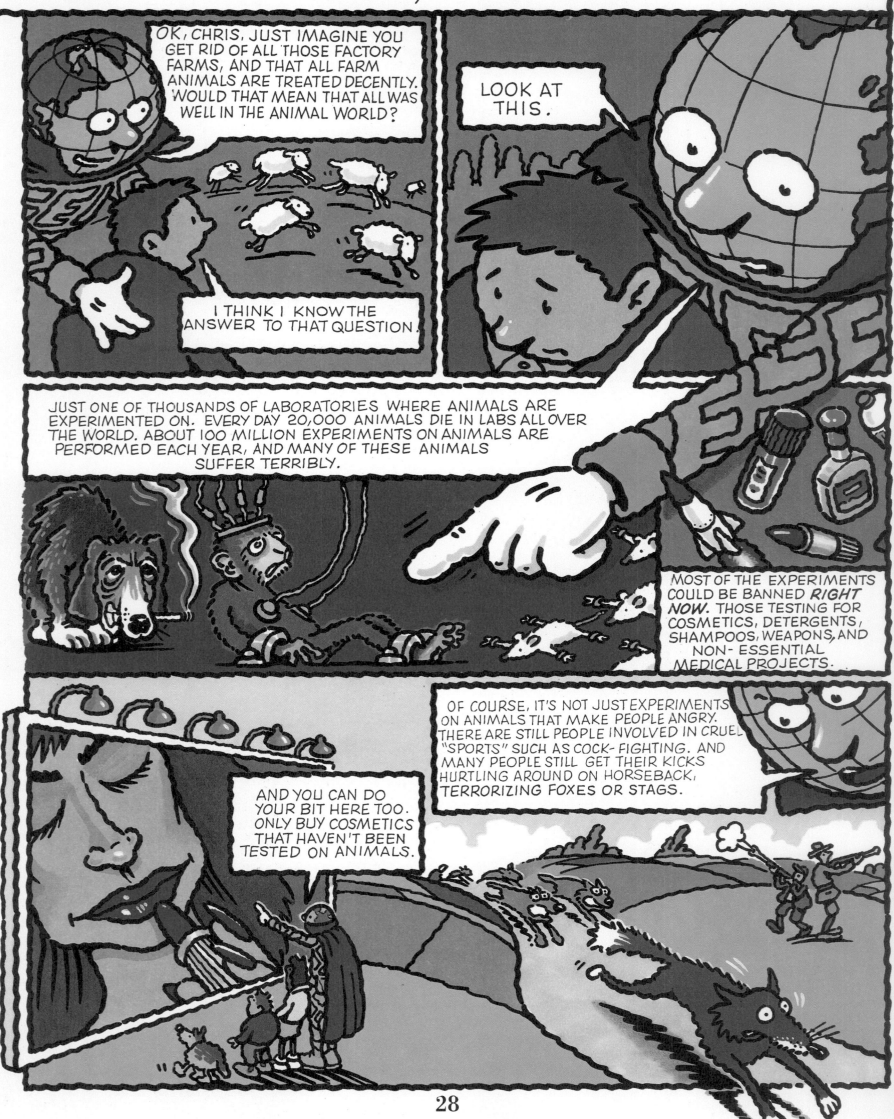

OK, CHRIS, JUST IMAGINE YOU GET RID OF ALL THOSE FACTORY FARMS, AND THAT ALL FARM ANIMALS ARE TREATED DECENTLY. WOULD THAT MEAN THAT ALL WAS WELL IN THE ANIMAL WORLD?

I THINK I KNOW THE ANSWER TO THAT QUESTION.

LOOK AT THIS.

JUST ONE OF THOUSANDS OF LABORATORIES WHERE ANIMALS ARE EXPERIMENTED ON. EVERY DAY 20,000 ANIMALS DIE IN LABS ALL OVER THE WORLD. ABOUT 100 MILLION EXPERIMENTS ON ANIMALS ARE PERFORMED EACH YEAR, AND MANY OF THESE ANIMALS SUFFER TERRIBLY.

MOST OF THE EXPERIMENTS COULD BE BANNED *RIGHT NOW*. THOSE TESTING FOR COSMETICS, DETERGENTS, SHAMPOOS, WEAPONS, AND NON-ESSENTIAL MEDICAL PROJECTS.

OF COURSE, IT'S NOT JUST EXPERIMENTS ON ANIMALS THAT MAKE PEOPLE ANGRY. THERE ARE STILL PEOPLE INVOLVED IN CRUEL "SPORTS" SUCH AS COCK-FIGHTING. AND MANY PEOPLE STILL GET THEIR KICKS HURTLING AROUND ON HORSEBACK, TERRORIZING FOXES OR STAGS.

AND YOU CAN DO YOUR BIT HERE TOO. ONLY BUY COSMETICS THAT HAVEN'T BEEN TESTED ON ANIMALS.

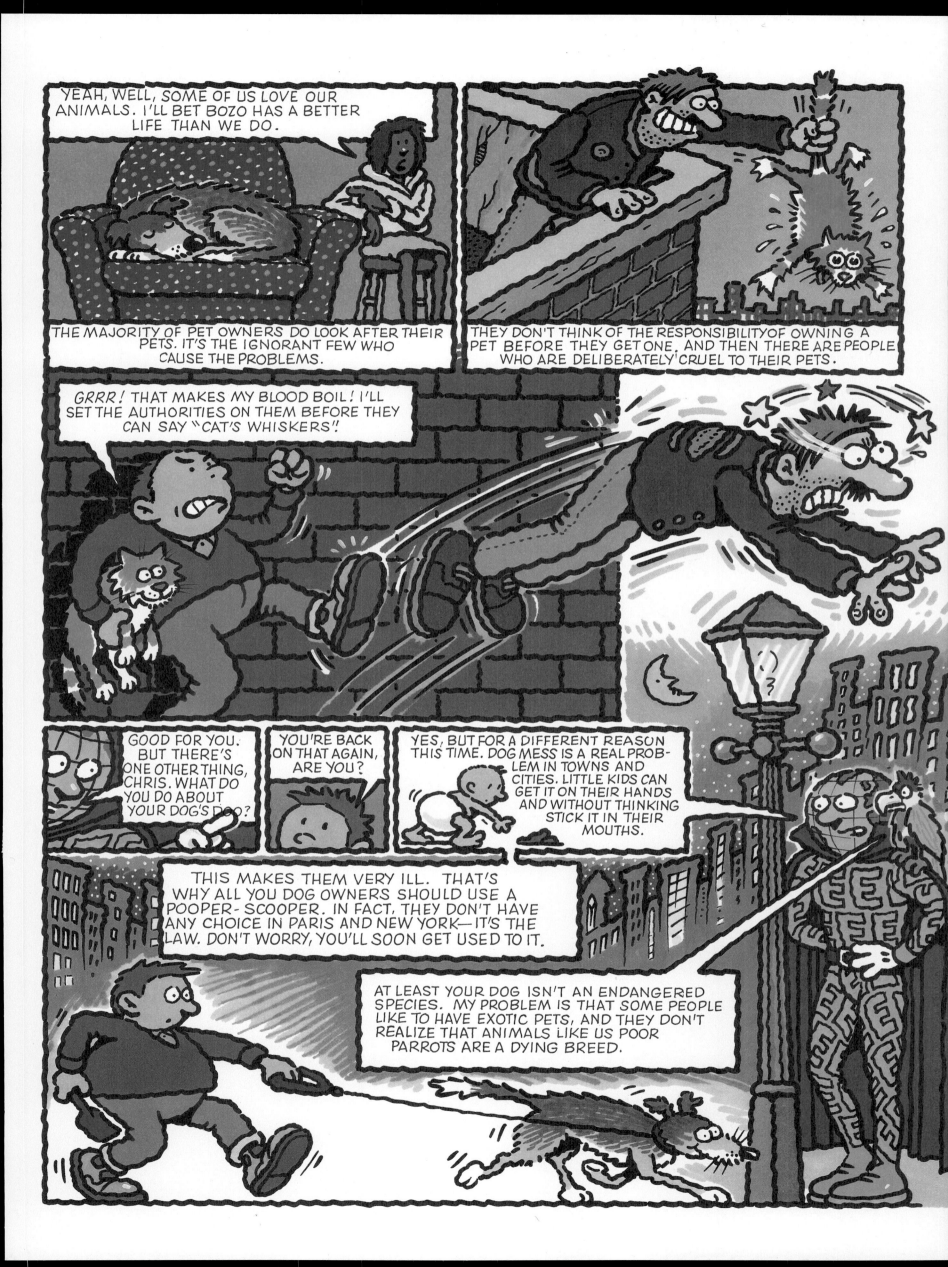

EXTINCTION IS FOREVER

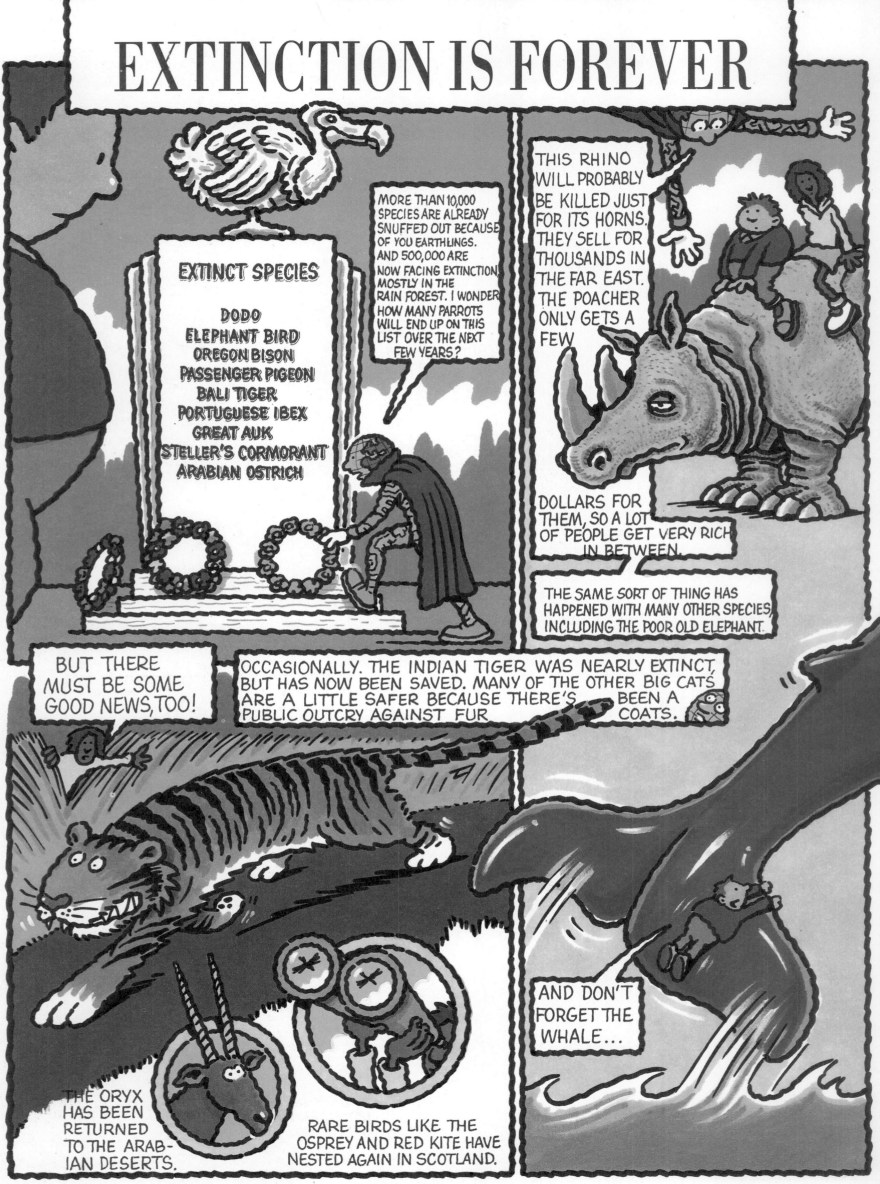

EXTINCT SPECIES

DODO
ELEPHANT BIRD
OREGON BISON
PASSENGER PIGEON
BALI TIGER
PORTUGUESE IBEX
GREAT AUK
STELLER'S CORMORANT
ARABIAN OSTRICH

MORE THAN 10,000 SPECIES ARE ALREADY SNUFFED OUT BECAUSE OF YOU EARTHLINGS. AND 500,000 ARE NOW FACING EXTINCTION, MOSTLY IN THE RAIN FOREST. I WONDER HOW MANY PARROTS WILL END UP ON THIS LIST OVER THE NEXT FEW YEARS?

THIS RHINO WILL PROBABLY BE KILLED JUST FOR ITS HORNS. THEY SELL FOR THOUSANDS IN THE FAR EAST. THE POACHER ONLY GETS A FEW DOLLARS FOR THEM, SO A LOT OF PEOPLE GET VERY RICH IN BETWEEN.

THE SAME SORT OF THING HAS HAPPENED WITH MANY OTHER SPECIES, INCLUDING THE POOR OLD ELEPHANT.

BUT THERE MUST BE SOME GOOD NEWS, TOO!

OCCASIONALLY. THE INDIAN TIGER WAS NEARLY EXTINCT, BUT HAS NOW BEEN SAVED. MANY OF THE OTHER BIG CATS ARE A LITTLE SAFER BECAUSE THERE'S BEEN A PUBLIC OUTCRY AGAINST FUR COATS.

THE ORYX HAS BEEN RETURNED TO THE ARABIAN DESERTS.

RARE BIRDS LIKE THE OSPREY AND RED KITE HAVE NESTED AGAIN IN SCOTLAND.

AND DON'T FORGET THE WHALE...

GOING, GOING ... SAVED!

THAT'S WHY THE WORLD'S REMAINING RAIN FORESTS ARE SO IMPORTANT. BECAUSE THEY ARE SWARMING WITH LIFE. SCIENTISTS ESTIMATE THAT ABOUT 60% OF ALL THE SPECIES ON EARTH CAN BE FOUND IN THE RAIN FORESTS. AND NOT JUST THE WELL-KNOWN ONES (*LIKE JAGUARS AND PARROTS*), BUT MILLIONS OF TINY CREATURES SUCH AS ANTS, TERMITES, FUNGI, CENTIPEDES, AND BEETLES.

YECH! I HATE BEETLES.

YOU MAY HATE THEM, BUT THEY'RE JUST AS IMPORTANT AS ANY OTHER CREATURE. ALL TOLD, MANY THOUSANDS OF INSECTS ARE BECOMING EXTINCT EVERY YEAR. THAT'S HOW FAST THE FORESTS ARE BEING DESTROYED. AND WITHIN 10 YEARS, ONE SPECIES COULD BE "POPPING ITS CLOGS" EVERY HOUR OF EVERY DAY. THE MIND IS POSITIVELY BOGGLED AT THE IDEA OF SUCH DESTRUCTION.

CHEER UP, ECO-FREAK. IT CAN'T BE THAT BAD.

BUT IT IS! MORE THAN HALF THE WORLD'S RAIN-FOREST HAS BEEN DESTROYED IN THE LAST 50 YEARS. YOU EARTHLINGS DON'T EVEN KNOW WHAT YOU'RE DESTROYING BEFORE IT'S GONE.

BEFORE

NOW

UNLIKE A LOT OF ENVIRONMENTAL DAMAGE, THIS CAN'T BE REVERSED. ONCE IT'S GONE, IT'S GONE. SURE, YOU CAN PLANT NEW TREES, BUT YOU CAN NEVER RECREATE ALL THE LOST ANIMAL AND PLANT SPECIES.

TIME IS RUNNING OUT FOR THE RAIN FORESTS. UNLESS YOU ACT NOW, THERE JUST WON'T BE ANY FOREST LEFT TO WORRY ABOUT IN THE NEXT CENTURY. AND EVERY ONE OF YOU WILL BE WORSE OFF AS A RESULT

LET ALONE THE BEETLES...

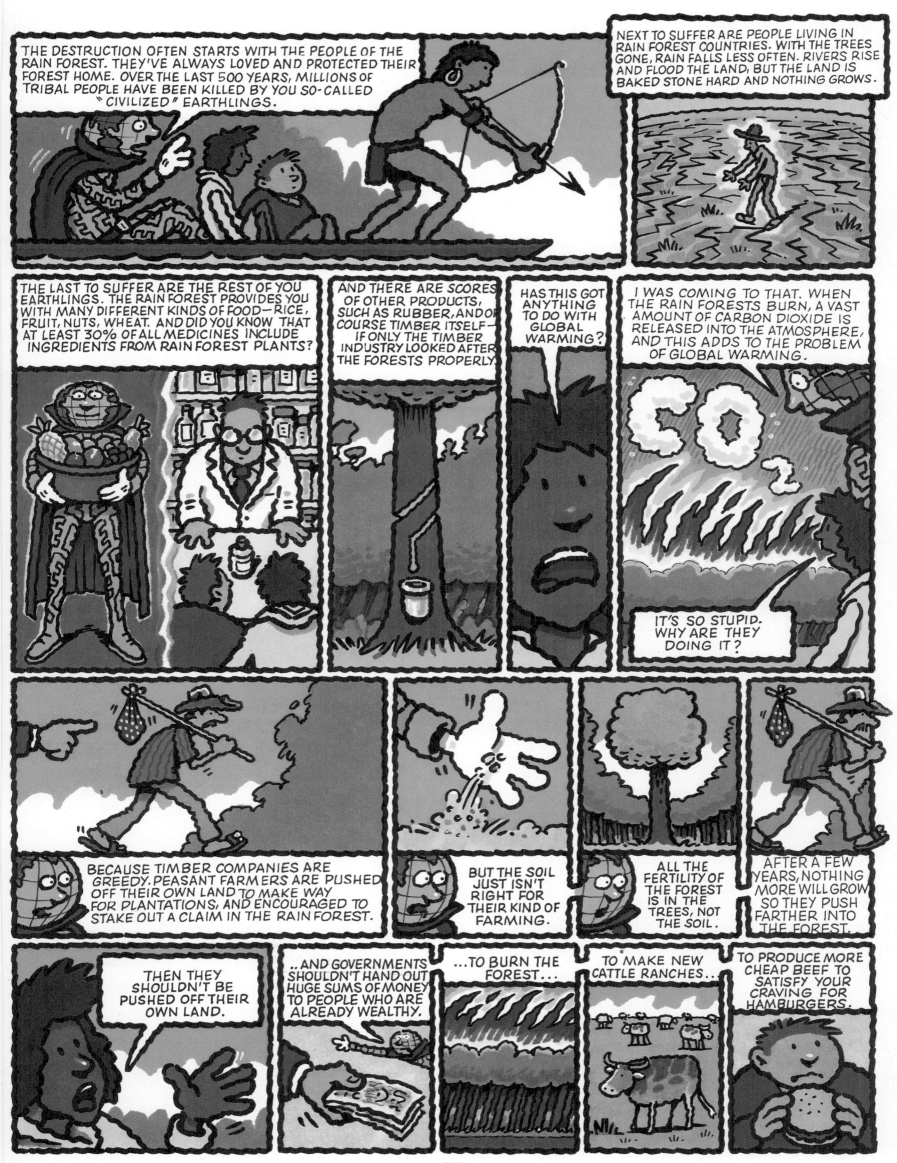

THE DESTRUCTION OFTEN STARTS WITH THE PEOPLE OF THE RAIN FOREST. THEY'VE ALWAYS LOVED AND PROTECTED THEIR FOREST HOME. OVER THE LAST 500 YEARS, MILLIONS OF TRIBAL PEOPLE HAVE BEEN KILLED BY YOU SO-CALLED "CIVILIZED" EARTHLINGS.

NEXT TO SUFFER ARE PEOPLE LIVING IN RAIN FOREST COUNTRIES. WITH THE TREES GONE, RAIN FALLS LESS OFTEN. RIVERS RISE AND FLOOD THE LAND, BUT THE LAND IS BAKED STONE HARD AND NOTHING GROWS.

THE LAST TO SUFFER ARE THE REST OF YOU EARTHLINGS. THE RAIN FOREST PROVIDES YOU WITH MANY DIFFERENT KINDS OF FOOD—RICE, FRUIT, NUTS, WHEAT. AND DID YOU KNOW THAT AT LEAST 30% OF ALL MEDICINES INCLUDE INGREDIENTS FROM RAIN FOREST PLANTS?

AND THERE ARE SCORES OF OTHER PRODUCTS, SUCH AS RUBBER, AND OF COURSE TIMBER ITSELF—IF ONLY THE TIMBER INDUSTRY LOOKED AFTER THE FORESTS PROPERLY.

HAS THIS GOT ANYTHING TO DO WITH GLOBAL WARMING?

I WAS COMING TO THAT. WHEN THE RAIN FORESTS BURN, A VAST AMOUNT OF CARBON DIOXIDE IS RELEASED INTO THE ATMOSPHERE, AND THIS ADDS TO THE PROBLEM OF GLOBAL WARMING.

CO_2

IT'S SO STUPID. WHY ARE THEY DOING IT?

BECAUSE TIMBER COMPANIES ARE GREEDY. PEASANT FARMERS ARE PUSHED OFF THEIR OWN LAND TO MAKE WAY FOR PLANTATIONS, AND ENCOURAGED TO STAKE OUT A CLAIM IN THE RAIN FOREST.

BUT THE SOIL JUST ISN'T RIGHT FOR THEIR KIND OF FARMING.

ALL THE FERTILITY OF THE FOREST IS IN THE TREES, NOT THE SOIL.

AFTER A FEW YEARS, NOTHING MORE WILL GROW SO THEY PUSH FARTHER INTO THE FOREST.

THEN THEY SHOULDN'T BE PUSHED OFF THEIR OWN LAND.

..AND GOVERNMENTS SHOULDN'T HAND OUT HUGE SUMS OF MONEY TO PEOPLE WHO ARE ALREADY WEALTHY.

...TO BURN THE FOREST...

TO MAKE NEW CATTLE RANCHES...

TO PRODUCE MORE CHEAP BEEF TO SATISFY YOUR CRAVING FOR HAMBURGERS.

33

AND THEY SHOULDN'T LET THE TIMBER COMPANIES DESTROY THE FORESTS WITH NO THOUGHT FOR FUTURE GENERATIONS.

MANY OF THE RAIN FOREST COUNTRIES ARE TRAPPED BY THE HUGE DEBTS THEY OWE TO RICH COUNTRIES LIKE YOURS. THEY CASH IN THEIR NATURAL WEALTH...

TO KEEP *YOUR* BANK MANAGERS HAPPY. THEY HAVEN'T A HOPE OF PAYING OFF THOSE DEBTS, BUT THE FORESTS ARE BEING CUT DOWN ANYWAY.

IT'S SO DEPRESSING.

DON'T DESPAIR. WITH A BIT OF VISION AND COMMITMENT, EVEN YOUR POLITICIANS COULD PUT TOGETHER A RESCUE PACKAGE. THINK OF THE RAIN FOREST AS THREE CIRCLES. THE INNER CIRCLE MUST BE PROTECTED *COMPLETELY*, AS BIOLOGICAL RESERVES. ONLY RESEARCH WOULD TAKE PLACE THERE.

THE RAIN FOREST INDIANS WOULD BE GIVEN CONTROL OF THESE AREAS, SINCE THEY UNDERSTAND HOW THE FOREST WORKS BETTER THAN ALL THE WESTERN SCIENTISTS PUT TOGETHER.

CHIEF PAIAKAN OF THE KAIAPO INDIANS IN BRAZIL SAYS:

"I SPEAK AS A PERSON WHO HAS LIVED ALL HIS LIFE IN THE FOREST. WITHOUT THE FOREST, WE HAVE NO LIFE...

WITHOUT THE FOREST, WE WON'T BE ABLE TO BREATHE, OUR HEARTS WILL STOP AND WE WILL DIE.

WE ARE SIMPLY TRYING TO SAVE THE KNOWLEDGE THAT THE FORESTS AND THIS PLANET ARE STILL *ALIVE*, AND GIVE IT BACK TO YOU WHO HAVE LOST THE WAY."

COLOMBIA, A COUNTRY IN SOUTH AMERICA, HAS SHOWN THE WAY.

CONTROL OF AN AREA OF 50 MILLION ACRES HAS BEEN HANDED BACK TO THE FOREST PEOPLE.

YOUR BONEHEAD BANKERS SHOULD CANCEL THE DEBTS OF RAIN FOREST COUNTRIES IN RETURN FOR SETTING UP THE BIOLOGICAL RESERVES. THE BANKS WON'T LOSE MUCH.

THEY KNOW ALREADY THAT THE DEBTS CAN'T BE PAID BACK.

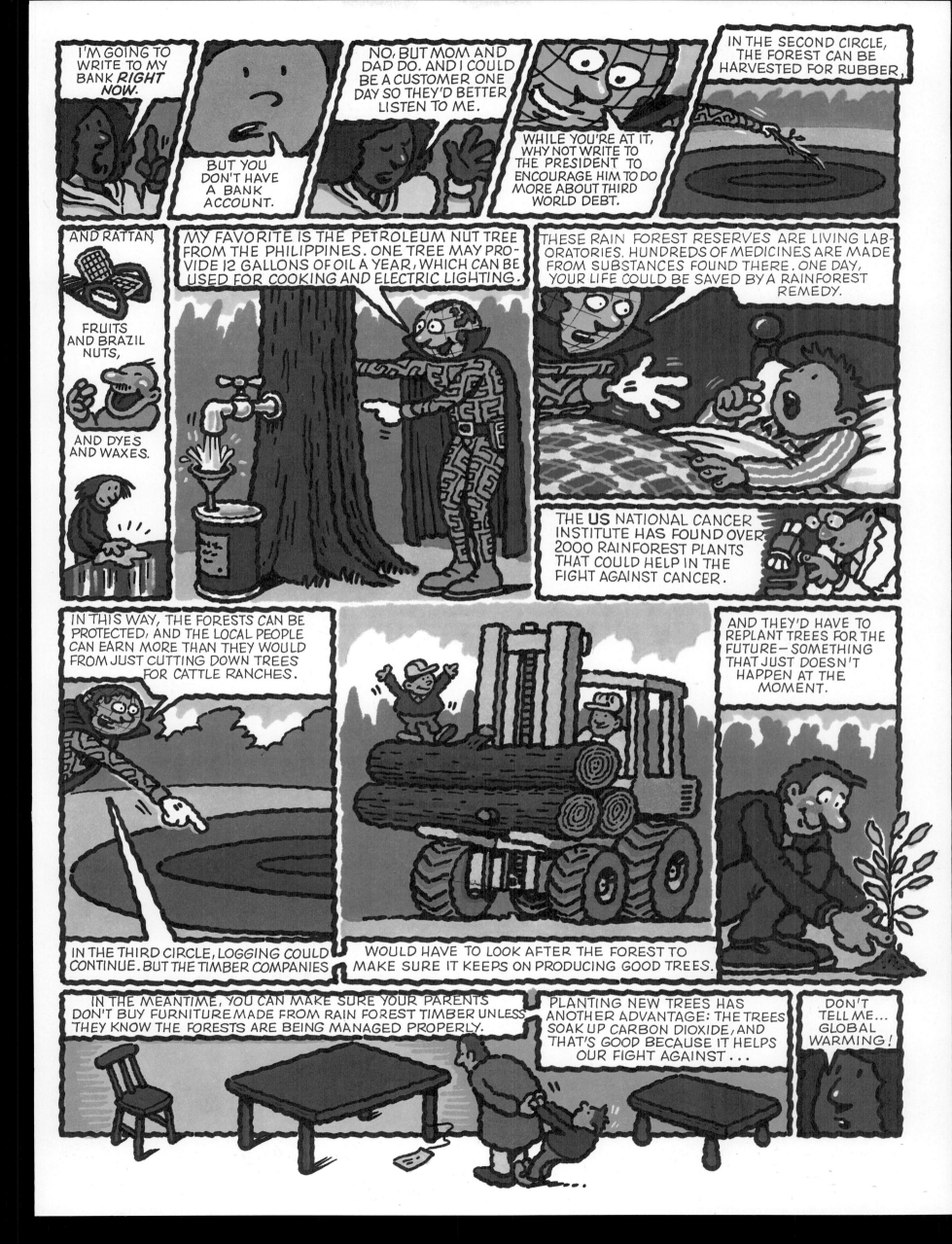

WARMING WARNING

BEYOND THE O-ZONE

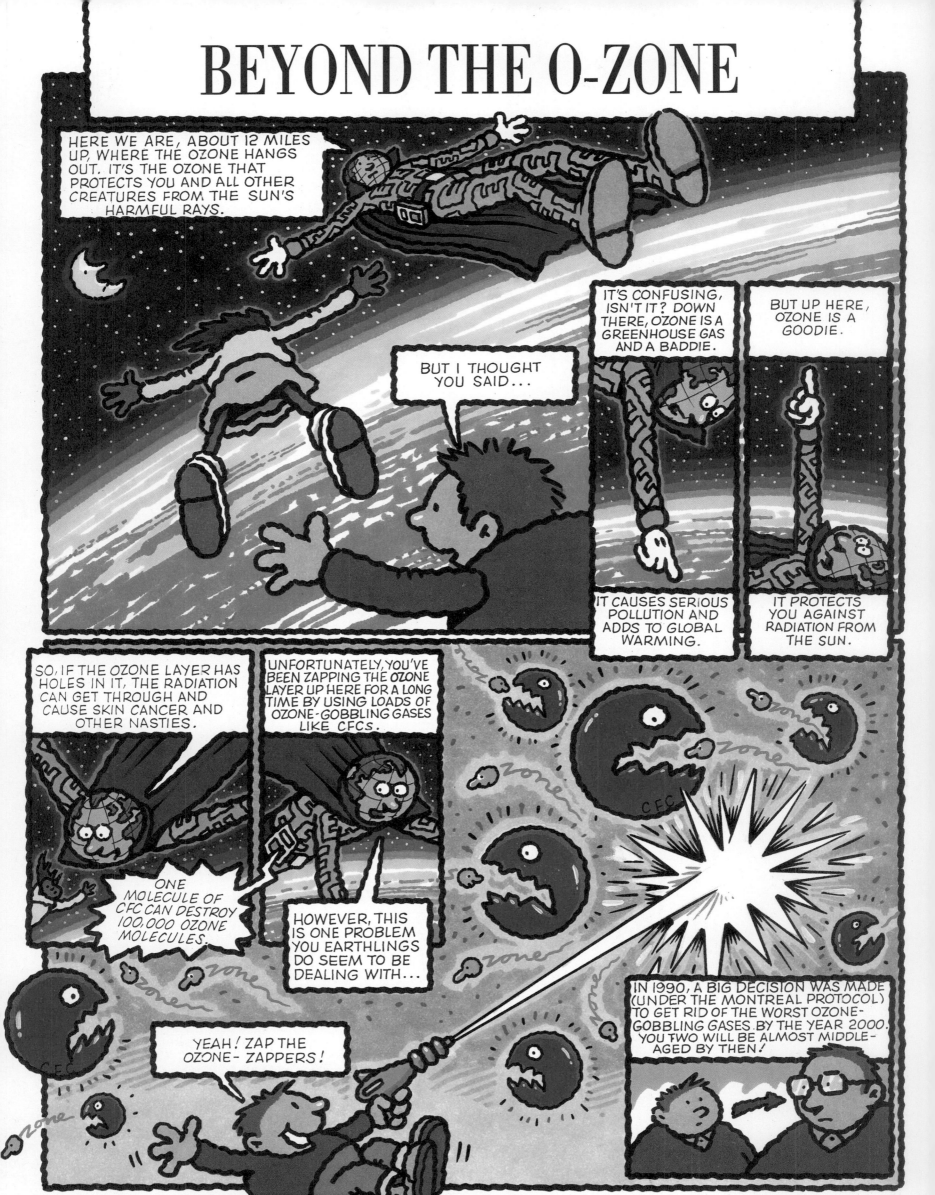

5.2 BILLON AND RISING

DEAD-END DEVELOPMENT

YOU SEE, THERE'S A BIG DIFFERENCE

BETWEEN GOOD DEVELOPMENT AND BAD DEVELOPMENT.

I THINK IT'S TIME YOU MET SOME OF...

YOUR BROTHERS AND SISTERS.

THIS IS JOSÉ AND MARIA.

THEY'VE GOT FOUR BROTHERS AND SISTERS. THEY HAD SIX, BUT TWO DIED—ONE FROM DYSENTERY, ONE FROM MALARIA.

THEIR FATHER USED TO OWN A SMALL FARM. LIFE WAS HARD, BUT THEY GOT BY. THEN, FIVE YEARS AGO, THEY WERE FORCED TO SELL THEIR LAND TO A BIG AMERICAN PINEAPPLE COMPANY.

THEIR DAD WAS PROMISED A JOB ON THE SAME LAND.

FOR 2 YEARS HE WORKED AS A LABORER, GROWING PINEAPPLES.

ONE DAY HE WAS TOLD THERE WAS NO MORE WORK.

HE HEARD THE GOVERNMENT WAS GIVING MONEY TO PEOPLE TO MOVE INTO THE FOREST TO BURN THE TREES AND PLANT CROPS. JOSÉ AND MARIA'S FAMILY AND THOUSANDS OF OTHER FAMILIES, TOOK THE MONEY AND WENT TO THE FOREST.

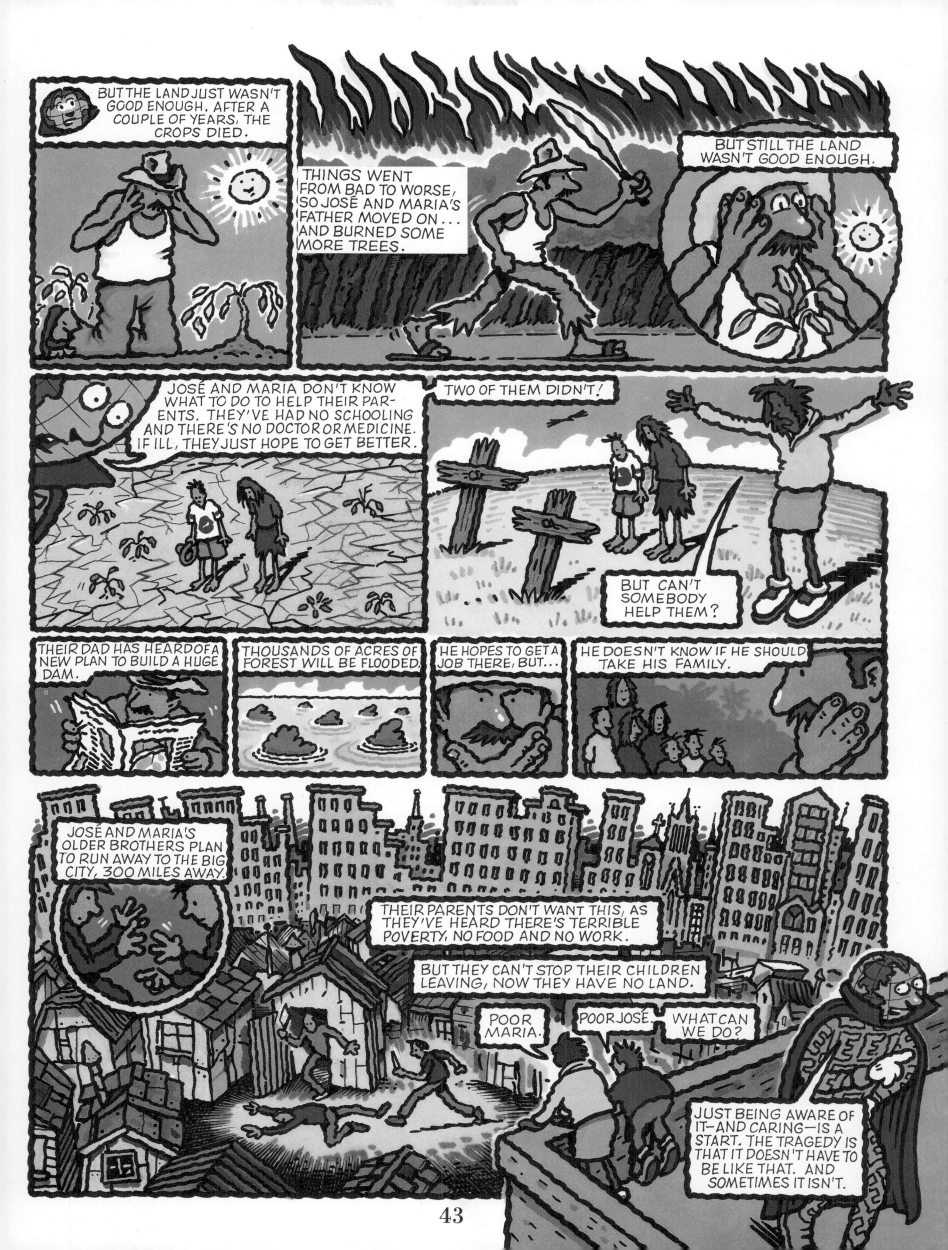

43

DEVELOPMENT WITH A FUTURE

LET'S SEE HOW IT CAN BE DONE.

THEIR PARENTS ALSO OWN A SMALL FARM

ON IT THEY GROW ALL SORTS OF FRUIT AND VEGETABLES, SOME FOR THEMSELVES AND SOME FOR SALE.

THIS IS HANIF AND ZINA. THEY'RE NOT MUCH BETTER OFF THAN JOSÉ AND MARIA, BUT IN EVERY OTHER WAY THEY COULD BE LIVING ON A DIFFERENT PLANET.

THEY ALSO KEEP A COUPLE OF PIGS AND SOME COWS, AS WELL AS THE CHICKENS AND DUCKS.

ALL THE FARMERS IN THE AREA SHARE MACHINERY, AND HELP EACH OTHER TO GROW AND SELL PINEAPPLES.

THEY OWN A SMALL CANNING FACTORY TOO—WHICH MEANS THEY CAN EARN MORE MONEY FROM THE PINEAPPLES.

HANIF AND ZINA HELP OUT ON THE FARM.

THEY ALSO GO TO SCHOOL, JUST LIKE YOU TWO.

HANIF CAN'T REALLY SEE THE POINT OF IT. HE JUST WANTS TO TAKE OVER THE FARM.

BUT ZINA WANTS TO BE A LOCAL HEALTH WORKER.

THEIR GOVERNMENT HAS THREE PRIORITIES:

1. EDUCATION
2. HEALTH-CARE.
3. LOCAL DEVELOP-MENT.

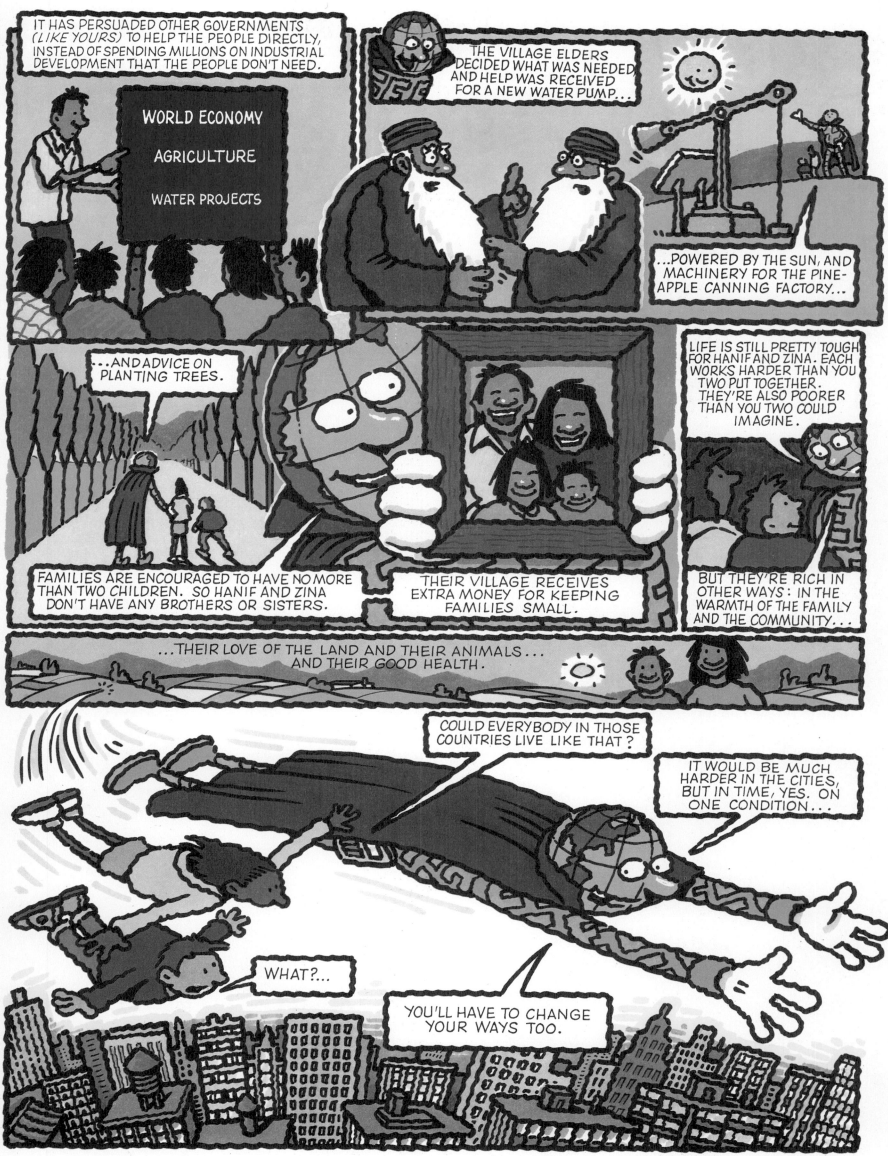

THE EARTH NEEDS YOU!

OR YOU CAN WORK TOWARD A BETTER WORLD, BY STARTING TO: PROTECT THE EARTH'S RICHES, CUT POLLUTION AND WASTE EVEN IF IT MEANS CONSUMING LESS, PLANT MORE TREES, THINK OF PROGRESS IN TERMS OF HAPPINESS AND JUSTICE FOR EVERYONE,...

RESPECT OTHER CREATURES AS HAVING VALUES IN THEIR OWN RIGHT, NOT JUST BECAUSE THEY'RE USEFUL TO YOU, SHARE YOUR WEALTH WITH POORER COUNTRIES.

GROWN-UPS TODAY JUST HAVEN'T BEEN ABLE TO MAKE THAT CHOICE. THE EARTH AND ALL ITS CREATURES HAVE BEEN BADLY DAMAGED AS A RESULT.

BUT THERE'S A NEW FORCE AT WORK IN THE WORLD. THINGS ARE CHANGING VERY FAST, AND IT'S TIME FOR YOU YOUNG EARTHLINGS TO MAKE PEACE WITH THE EARTH. WILL YOU HELP ME?

LEAVE IT TO US, CAPTAIN ECO. THE EARTH'S IN GOOD HANDS NOW.

CAN'T YOU STAY? WHY NOT TAKE MOM AND DAD ON THE SAME TRIP?

I'LL LEAVE THAT TO YOU. BUT DON'T WORRY. I'LL BE BACK TO SEE HOW YOU'RE GETTING ON.

I'M NEVER FAR AWAY, AS YOU'LL FIND OUT. I'M JUST A SMALL PART OF THE SPIRIT OF THE EARTH.

THAT SPIRIT IS IN EVERY ONE OF YOU.

AND IT'S UP TO YOU TO KEEP IT ALIVE.

47

OVER TO YOU, EARTHLINGS...

As you've seen, the bad news is that the Earth is in trouble. The good news is that you can do a lot to help, at home and at school. Write letters to politicians, find out as much as you can, join an organization, set up a fund-raising group, stop buying things you don't really need. Here is a checklist of things to remember.

SAVE ENERGY
• Remember to turn off the lights when you're not in the room.
• Persuade your parents to try out the new, energy-efficient lightbulbs.
• Find out how well insulated your home is - the less energy you use as a family, the more money your parents will save!
• Switch off the TV from the set, not by remote control.

TRAVEL GREEN
• Walk, bicycle, or use public transport-ation whenever you can.
• Make sure your parents' car uses unleaded gas and gets as many miles to the gallon as possible.
• Find out more about catalytic converters. It might be possible for your parents to have one installed in their car.

REDUCE, REPAIR, REUSE, RECYCLE
• Recycle paper, cans, and bottles that might otherwise get thrown away.
• Use recycled paper, and always reuse any plastic bags.
• Don't drop litter!
• Write, or get your parents to write, to state and local departments to find out more about recycling programs.
• Start a paper recycling program at school.
• Avoid disposable items; try to buy things that will last.

CAMPAIGN FOR ANIMAL RIGHTS
• Don't buy jewelry or accessories made from animal skins or ivory.
• Always preserve places where animals live, such as nests and burrows.
• Only buy cosmetics that are labeled cruelty-free (not tested on animals).

EAT HEALTHY FOOD
• Eat less junk food, and less meat.
• Eat plenty of fresh fruit and vegetables (preferably organically grown).
• Cut down on sugar by cutting down on candy, cookies, and soft drinks.

SAVE THE FORESTS
• Make sure your parents don't buy furniture or other goods made from tropical hardwoods, unless they come from properly managed forests. Find out more from Friends of the Earth (see right).
• Plant a tree for the future.

BAN CFCs
• Don't buy take-out food that comes in styrofoam containers - some of them contain CFCs, which are still harming the ozone layer.
• Avoid using aerosols if you can - and make sure they don't contain CFCs (the label should tell you).
• If your parents are getting rid of an old refrigerator, your local government should advise them on how to dispose of it without releasing CFCs into the environment.

DON'T WASTE WATER
• Water is precious! Don't flush the toilet more often than necessary, and don't leave the faucet running.

START YOUR OWN GROUP
The next thing you can do is get together with a group of friends and set up your own green group or action team. Help turn your school into the most environment-friendly place anywhere in the community.

FURTHER READING
Environment Skill Book (Boy Scouts of America)
Atlas of Enrironmental Issues by Nick Middleton (Facts on File)
Fifty Simple Things Kids Can do to Save the Earth by the Earth works Project Staff (Greenleaf)
Can the Whales be Saved? by Philip Whitfield (Viking Penguin)
Gertie's Green Thumb by Catherine Dexter (Macmillan)
The Changing Face of the Earth by D.C Money (Gareth Stevens Inc.)
Silent Spring by Rachel L. Carson (Houghton Mifflin)

ADDRESS FILE

When writing to organizations for information about environmental issues, enclose a large self-addressed stamped envelope.

Conservation International
1015 18th St, NW; Suite 1000
Washington, DC 20036

Cousteau Society
930 W. 21st Street
Norfolk, VA 23517

Cultural Survival, Inc.
11 Divinity Avenue
Cambridge, MA 02138

Friends of the Earth
218 D Street, SE
Washington, DC 20003

Greenpeace USA
1436 U Street, NW
Washington, DC 20009

International Rivers Network
301 Broadway, Suite B
San Francisco, CA 94133

National Audubon Society
950 Third Avenue
New York, NY 10022

National Geographic
P.O. Box 2895
Washington, DC 20077-9960

National Wildlife Federation
1412 16th Street, NW
Washington, DC 20036

Rainforest Action Network
301 Broadway, Suite A
San Francisco, CA 94133

World Wildlife Fund
1250 24th Street, NW
Washington, DC 20037